WHAT
DOUG the PUG®
TEACHES US

WHAT
DOUG the PUG®
TEACHES US

SIT, SPEAK, DO GOOD.

■ WILLOW CREEK PRESS®

Published by Willow Creek Press, Inc.
P.O. Box 147, Minocqua, Wisconsin 54548

All Photos © Leslie Mosier

Printed in China

REAL CHANGE, ENDURING CHANGE,
HAPPENS ONE STEP AT A TIME.
-RUTH BADER GINSBURG

SPEAK UP FOR THOSE WHO HAVE NO VOICE.

FIGHT FOR THE THINGS THAT YOU CARE ABOUT,
BUT DO IT IN A WAY THAT WILL LEAD
OTHERS TO JOIN YOU.
-RUTH BADER GINSBURG

IN EVERY WALK WITH NATURE ONE
RECEIVES FAR MORE THAN HE SEEKS.
-JOHN MUIR

GET IN TOUCH WITH NATURE.

IN NATURE NOTHING IS PERFECT AND EVERYTHING IS PERFECT.
-ALICE WALKER

LOVE THE WORLD AS YOUR SELF; THEN YOU CAN TRULY CARE FOR ALL THINGS.
-LAO TZU

CHOOSE ONLY ONE MASTER -
NATURE.
-REMBRANDT

IF ONE HAS COURAGE, NOTHING CAN DIM THE LIGHT THAT SHINES FROM WITHIN.
-MAYA ANGELOU

BE A RAINBOW IN SOMEONE ELSE'S CLOUD.
-BOB GOFF

THE BEST WAY TO CHEER YOURSELF IS TO TRY TO CHEER SOMEONE ELSE UP.
-MARK TWAIN

DO OR DO NOT, THERE IS NO TRY.
-YODA

THE GREATEST TEACHER, FAILURE IS.
-HENRY FORD

EDUCATION IS NOT THE FILLING OF A POT BUT THE LIGHTING OF A FIRE.
-W.B. YEATS

INDIFFERENCE AND NEGLECT OFTEN DO MUCH
MORE DAMAGE THAN OUTRIGHT DISLIKE.

-J.K. ROWLING

USE YOUR POWERS FOR GOOD, NOT EVIL.

IT MATTERS NOT WHAT SOMEONE IS BORN,
BUT WHAT THEY GROW TO BE.

-ALBUS DUMBLEDORE

IT'S NOT WHAT YOU LOOK AT THAT MATTERS, IT'S WHAT YOU SEE.
-HENRY DAVID THOREAU

KEEP YOUR EYES ON THE STARS AND YOUR FEET ON THE GROUND.
-BOBBY UNSER

SUCCESS COMES FROM HAVING DREAMS THAT ARE BIGGER THAN YOUR FEARS.

WE AIM ABOVE THE MARK TO HIT THE MARK.
-RALPH WALDO EMERSON

IT IS DURING OUR DARKEST MOMENTS THAT WE MUST FOCUS TO SEE THE LIGHT.
-ARISTOTLE ONASSIS

OUR GREATEST GLORY IS NOT IN NEVER FAILING,
BUT IN RISING UP EVERY TIME WE FAIL.
-RALPH WALDO EMERSON

HEAVEN IS   WE CAN DO

IF YOU STUMBLE
MAKE IT PART
OF THE DANCE.

ENOUGH.

HENRY DAVID THOREAU   -HELEN KELLER

TELL ME, WHAT IS IT YOU PLAN TO DO WITH
YOUR ONE WILD AND PRECIOUS LIFE?
-MARY OLIVER

I WANT TO LIVE IN A WORLD CREATED BY ART, NOT JUST DECORATED WITH IT.
-BANKSY

IF YOU WANT TO FLY, GIVE UP EVERYTHING THAT WEIGHS YOU DOWN.

IT ALWAYS SEEMS IMPOSSIBLE UNTIL IT'S DONE.
NELSON MANDELA

LIFE IS EITHER A DARING ADVENTURE OR NOTHING AT ALL.
HELEN KELLER

FEET, WHAT DO I NEED YOU FOR WHEN I HAVE WINGS TO FLY?
-FRIDA KAHLO

IF YOU SEE SOMETHING BEAUTIFUL
IN SOMEONE SPEAK IT.
-RUTHIE LINDSEY

SURROUND
YOURSELF WITH
PEOPLE THAT
ALLOW YOU
TO BLOOM.
-ANAIS NIN

EVERY FLOWER IS A SOUL
BLOSSOMING IN NATURE.
-GERARD DE NERVAL

LIFE IS UNCERTAIN. EAT DESSERT FIRST.
-ERNESTINE ULMER

ANYTHING

PEOPLE WHO

WORTH

LOVE TO EAT

IS WORTH

ARE ALWAYS

OVER

THE BEST

TREAT
YO'SELF.

PEOPLE.

-MICK JAGGER

-JULIA CHILD

TOO MUCH OF A GOOD THING
CAN BE WONDERFUL!
-MAE WEST

UNLESS SOMEONE LIKE YOU CARES A WHOLE AWFUL LOT, NOTHING IS GOING TO GET BETTER. IT'S NOT.
-DR. SEUSS

LEND A PAW TO THOSE IN NEED.

SERVICE TO OTHERS IS THE RENT YOU PAY FOR YOUR ROOM HERE ON EARTH.
-MUHAMMAD ALI

FOLLOW YOUR BLISS AND THE UNIVERSE WILL OPEN
DOORS WHERE THERE WERE ONLY WALLS.
-JOSEPH CAMPBELL

TH FREEDOM, MY BUSINESS IS
OKS, ENJOY AND HAV
ND THE MOON FUN AND WHY
HO COULD NOT THE EN
BE HAPPY? END, RIGHT?
-OSCAR WILDE -JANIS JOPLIN

DANCE UNTIL FLOWERS FALL OUT OF YOUR HAIR.

THE EARTH HAS MUSIC FOR
THOSE WHO LISTEN.
-WILLIAM SHAKESPEARE

NOW IS NO TIME TO THINK OF WHAT YOU DO NOT HAVE.
THINK OF WHAT YOU CAN DO WITH WHAT THERE IS.
-ERNEST HEMINGWAY

THE SECRET TO HAVING IT ALL IS KNOWING THAT YOU ALREADY DO.

-ROBERT BRAULT

WE SHOULD ALL BE THANKFUL FOR THOSE
PEOPLE WHO REKINDLE THE INNER SPIRIT.
-ALBERT SCHWEITZER

I REALLY DON'T THINK I NEED BUNS OF STEEL.
I'D BE HAPPY WITH BUNS OF CINNAMON.
-ELLEN DEGENERES

YOU DON'T   LIFE IS LIKE A

DON'T BE
EYE CANDY.
BE SOUL FOOD.

-PAUL PRUDHOMME

INGREDIENTS.

-UNKNOWN

LIFE IS TOO SHORT FOR FAKE
BUTTER OR FAKE PEOPLE.
-JULIA CHILD

A DOG IS THE ONLY THING ON THIS EARTH THAT
LOVES YOU MORE THAN HE LOVES HIMSELF.

- JOSH BILLINGS

A FRIEND IS   LOVE IS THAT
SOMEONE   CONDITION
KNOWS   IN WHICH THE
ABOUT YOU AND   HAPPINESS OF
                               ANOTHER PERSON
ALL LOVES YOU.   IS ESSENTIAL TO
                               YOUR OWN.

UNEXPECTED
KISSES ARE
THE BEST.

-ELBERT HUBBARD   -ROBERT A. HEINLEIN

BE THE PERSON YOUR DOG
THINKS YOU ARE.

-J.W. STEPHENS

WE COULD NEVER LEARN TO BE BRAVE AND PATIENT,
IF THERE WERE ONLY JOY IN THE WORLD.
-HELEN KELLER

THE DAY YOU PLANT THE SEED IS NOT THE DAY YOU EAT THE FRUIT.

HE THAT CAN HAVE PATIENCE
CAN HAVE WHAT HE WILL.
-BENJAMIN FRANKLIN

NOT EVERYTHING THAT WEIGHS
YOU DOWN IS YOURS TO CARRY.
-ANONYMOUS

TAKE ONLY A JOURNEY

DON'T CARRY
MEMORIES THOUSAND
WHAT YOU BEGIN
LEAVE ONLY WITH A
DON'T NEED.
FOOTPRINTS. SINGLE STEP

-CHIEF SEATTLE   -LAO TZU

THE MAN WHO MOVES A MOUNTAIN BEGINS
BY CARRYING AWAY SMALL STONES.
-CONFUCIUS

I REFUSE TO BELIEVE THAT YOU CANNOT BE
BOTH COMPASSIONATE AND STRONG.
-JACINDA ARDERN

THE THINGS   NORMAL IS NO
THAT MAKE ME   HING TO
DIFFERENT ARE   O, IT'
THE THINGS   NG TO
MAKE ME.   GET AWAY FRO

NO ONE IS YOU AND
THAT'S YOUR
SUPERPOWER.

-A. A. MILNE   -JODIE FOSTER

I AM STILL FIGHTING TO MAKE THE WORLD
A BETTER PLACE AND YOU CAN TOO.
-GABBY GIFFORDS

LIFE IS LIKE RIDING A BICYCLE, TO KEEP
YOUR BALANCE, YOU MUST KEEP MOVING.
-ALBERT EINSTEIN

THERE ARE
FAR, FAR
BETTER
THINGS
AHEAD
ANY
LEAVE
BEHIND.
-C. S. LEWIS

**DON'T
LOOK BACK.
YOU'RE NOT
GOING THAT
WAY.**

DON'T LET
YESTERDAY
TAKE UP TOO
MUCH OF
TODAY.
ANONYMOUS

IF YOU CAN'T FLY THEN RUN, IF YOU CAN'T RUN THEN WALK,
IF YOU CAN'T WALK THEN CRAWL, BUT WHATEVER YOU DO
YOU HAVE TO KEEP MOVING FORWARD.
-MARTIN LUTHER KING JR.

I DON'T LIKE TO GAMBLE, BUT IF THERE'S ONE THING I'M WILLING TO BET ON, IT'S MYSELF.

-BEYONCE

YOUR VALUE DOESN'T DECREASE BASED ON SOMEONE'S INABILITY TO SEE YOUR WORTH.

MANY RECEIVE ADVICE, ONLY THE WISE PROFIT FROM IT.

-HARPER LEE

NOBODY HAS EVER MEASURED, NOT EVEN POETS,
HOW MUCH THE HEART CAN HOLD.
-ZELDA FITZGERALD

SOMETIMES YOU NEED TO LOOK AT THINGS FROM A DIFFERENT PERSPECTIVE.

WHAT WE SEE DEPENDS MAINLY
ON WHAT WE LOOK FOR.
-JOHN LUBBOCK

YOU CAN DO WHAT I CANNOT DO. I CAN DO WHAT YOU CANNOT DO. TOGETHER WE CAN DO GREAT THINGS.
-MOTHER TERESA

A LOT OF DIFFERENT FLOWERS MAKE A BOUQUET.

-EDWARD... -LOUISA MAY ALCOTT

STRENGTH LIES IN DIFFERENCES, NOT IN SIMILARITIES.
-STEPHAN R. COVEY

THOSE THAT DON'T GOT IT, CAN'T SHOW IT.
THOSE THAT GOT IT, CAN'T HIDE IT.
-ZORA NEALE HURSTON

WHAT YOU
DO MAKES A
FFE
U HA
NHA
FFERENCE YOU
NT TO MAKE.
-JANE GOODALL

AN ARTIST IS
SOMEONE WHO

EMBRACE YOUR WEIRDNESS.

INTENTIONALL
AND REGULARL
-LISA CONGDON

DO ANYTHING, BUT LET IT PRODUCE JOY.
-WALT WHITMAN

ADOPT THE PACE OF NATURE, HER SECRET IS PATIENCE.

-JOHN BURROUGHS

NATURE DOES NOT HURRY, YET EVERYTHING IS ACCOMPLISHED.

-LAO TZU

-BUDDHA

WHEREVER YOU STAND, BE THE SOUL OF THAT PLACE.

-RUMI

LEARN FROM THE PAST, LOOK TO THE FUTURE, BUT LIVE IN THE PRESENT.
-PETRA NEMCOVA

WHEREVER YOU ARE BE ALL THERE.

DICKINSON

TODAY IS THE FIRST DAY OF THE REST OF YOUR LIFE.
-CHARLES DEDERICH

MAKE TIME TO CELEBRATE YOUR ACCOMPLISHMENTS.

DEEP SUMMER IS WHEN LAZINESS
FINDS RESPECTABILITY.
-SAM KEEN

IT'S A SMILE,

SUMMERTIME

IT'S A KISS,

KEEP CALM
AND FLOAT ON.

BEST OF WHAT

IT'S

SUMMERTIME!

-CHARLES BOWDEN

-KENNY CHESNEY

BUT TOMORROW MAY RAIN,
SO I'LL FOLLOW THE SUN.
-THE BEATLES

LIFE'S NOT ABOUT WAITING FOR THE STORM TO PASS...IT'S ABOUT LEARNING TO DANCE IN THE RAIN.

-VIVIAN GREENE

HE WAY I SEE IT, RAINY DAY
F YOU WHEN IT ILD B
RAINBOW SPENT AT HO
GOT TO WHEN IT CUP
WITH A RAINS, LOOK AND A G
FOR RAINBOWS.

-DOLLY PARTON -BILL WATTERS

THE BEST THING ONE CAN DO WHEN IT'S RAINING IS TO LET IT RAIN.

-HENRY WADSWORTH LONGFELLOW

WHEN WE'RE IN CHARGE OF OUR OWN STORIES,
AMAZING THINGS HAPPEN.
-AWKWAFINA

SURROUND YOURSELF WITH THE PEOPLE THAT MAKE YOUR HEART SMILE.

I ALWAYS WONDERED WHY SOMEBODY
DOESN'T DO SOMETHING ABOUT THAT.
THEN I REALIZED I WAS SOMEBODY.
-LILY TOMLIN

NEVER DULL YOUR SHINE FOR ANYONE ELSE.
-TYRA BANKS

TAKE CARE OF YOUR BODY. IT'S THE ONLY PLACE THAT YOU HAVE TO LIVE.

I DON'T BELIEVE IN GUILTY PLEASURES. IF YOU ENJOY SOMETHING, THERE'S NOTHING GUILTY ABOUT IT.
-BUSY PHILLIPS

FAILURE IS A **BRUISE** NOT A TATTOO.

WE ARE NOT WHAT OTHER PEOPLE SAY WE ARE. WE ARE WHO
WE KNOW OURSELVES TO BE, AND WE ARE WHAT WE LOVE.
-LAVERNE COX

DON'T BE AFRAID TO SHOW YOUR TRUE COLORS.

-MARILYN MONROE

FIGURE OUT WHO YOU ARE,
THEN DO IT ON PURPOSE.
-DOLLY PARTON

DOGS DO SPEAK, BUT ONLY TO THOSE
WHO KNOW HOW TO LISTEN.
-ORHAN PAMUK

TO ERR IS HUMAN, TO FORGIVE IS CANINE.

I NEED TO LISTEN WELL SO THAT
I HEAR WHAT IS NOT SAID.
-THULI MADONSELA

THERE IS NO ONE-SIZE-FITS-ALL NARRATIVE;
EVERYONE'S PATH WINDS IN DIFFERENT WAYS.
-SARAH MCBRIDE

EXPECT NOTHING.
LIVE FRUGALLY
ON SURPRISE.
-RALPH WALDO EMERSON

YOU ARE WHAT YOU BELIEVE
YOURSELF TO BE.
-PAULO COELHO

A RIGHT IS NOT WHAT SOMEONE GIVES YOU;
IT'S WHAT NO ONE CAN TAKE AWAY FROM YOU.
-RAMSEY CLARK

KNOW YOUR POWER.

-STACEY ABRAMS -ALEXANDRIA OCASIO-C

OUR UNITY IS OUR STRENGTH
AND DIVERSITY IS OUR POWER.
-KAMALA HARRIS

THERE MIGHT BE DAYS WHERE YOU SAY, 'I CAN'T. I CAN'T EVEN.' BUT YOU CAN. YOU CAN EVEN.
-KATIE COURIC

EVERYTHING YOU WANT IS ON THE OTHER SIDE OF FEAR.

-TONY ROBBINS

CHALLENGES MAKE YOU DISCOVER THINGS ABOUT YOURSELF THAT YOU NEVER REALLY KNEW.
-CICELY TYSON

WHEN I BELIEVE IN SOMETHING,
I'M LIKE A DOG WITH A BONE.
-MELISSA MCCARTHY

I TRAIN TO BE   THE ONLY
THE BEST   PERSON WHO CAN
THE WORLD   STOP YOU FROM
             REACHING YOUR
WORK HARD GOALS IS YOU.
REST HARDER.
WORST DAY.
             -JACKIE
-RONDA ROUSEY   JOYNER-KERSEE

BOSS UP AND CHANGE YOUR LIFE.
YOU CAN HAVE IT ALL, NO SACRIFICE.
-LIZZO

THERE IS ALWAYS LIGHT, IF ONLY WE'RE BRAVE ENOUGH
TO SEE IT. IF ONLY WE'RE BRAVE ENOUGH TO BE IT...
-AMANDA GORMAN

THERE ARE BY BEING
TWO WAYS OF YOURSELF,
SPREAD YOU PUT
TO BE THE CANDLE SOMETHING
OR THE WONDERFUL
THAT REFLECTS THE WORLD
THAT WAS NOT
HERE BEFORE
-EDITH WHARTON -EDWIN ELLIOT

SHINE BRIGHT, BE THE LIGHT.

FIND YOUR LIGHT; THEY CAN'T
LOVE YOU IF THEY CAN'T SEE YOU.
-BETTE MIDLER